Meditating with Aromatic

A Unique Interactive Project

by Vivienne Tuffnell

1

Meditating with Aromatics

Meditating with Aromatics

Introduction to the First Volume

This is unashamedly a work in progress and an experiment in exploring some of the possibilities in the new digital media explosion. Charles Dickens published his novels in instalments that had people eager for each new episode of the stories he wove, and remembering this I wondered if perhaps today we are too eager to sample only a finished work.

Perhaps we are too used to simply receiving passively rather than actively getting involved. I've seen a number of projects online that aim to be interactive and it intrigues me: can the audience influence and change a project in such a way that their input enhances the finished product? I've always been wary of sharing any details of my fiction for the reason that the ideas of another can irretrievably alter the course of a story.

However, this project is deliberately intended for the readers to interact with the product. That is not to say I wish for help or assistance, but rather that the readers may(or may not) choose to participate in the creation. It works like this:

This is a preliminary booklet of a project I have been working on for some time, writing short guided meditations to be used with various aromatic substances. The booklet will be available both as a download and as a hard copy, at as low a price as I can manage. If you are reading this then you have chosen one or other method of obtaining it. Now having read this booklet, think about what aromatic substances you would like to have a meditation written for. Are they on my list in the table of contents? If they are or if they are not, I'd really love it if you would contact me at viviennetuffnell@hotmail.co.uk and let me know which you would love, which you would hate and anything else that strikes you. I am open to suggestions and to feedback. I'd also like to gather a small

Meditating with Aromatics

group of people who would like to use these meditations and to gather personal stories from them from what occurred during their explorations. Identities would be kept private but the feedback from this would be of great use in shaping future meditations.

The meditations included here have appeared also at my blog http://zenandtheartoftightropewalking.wordpress.com and have been well received. One of the reasons why it is taking me so long to produce these meditations is simply a sense of reluctance. Why go to the effort of producing a book that few if any might want to read? The feedback I have gathered so far is that enough people would want such a book, and therefore I have begun the project. Your input as reader and meditator is likely to be of great power in shaping and directing the book.

Finally, I'd just like to add that as the book grows I intend to release it in instalments and finally, once the whole project is completed, make a single volume available (while perhaps leaving the stages also available.) It's going to be messy, but all acts of creation are: we only tend to see the cleaned-up baby smelling of soap and sleeping peacefully.

So dive in and try the meditations out, have fun, and see what else you'd like to see in the book. It's an experiment; let's see what we discover together.

Vivienne Tuffnell May 2011

Meditating with Aromatics

Provisional List of Contents

Introduction: About this Book

Who it is aimed at and why has it been written. How to use the book

Chapter One: Introduction to Meditation

History, cultures, benefits, spirituality etc.

Chapter Two: Introduction to Aromatics

What are aromatics, history of the use of aromatics through time, science of aromatherapy, limbic system etc, benefits of using aroma in daily life etc.

Methods of use (*incense, vaporisation, smelling strips etc.*)

Chapter Three: Basics of Meditation:

Posture, setting, timing, breathing, music etc.

How to use the guided meditations

Preparations, relaxation, grounding, recording of experiences

Chapter Four: Everyday Aromatics

Using ordinary and familiar scents to deepen meditation

May include: Orange, chocolate, coffee, bread, mint, lavender, vanilla, rosemary, apple, honey, aniseed, strawberries, pine cones,

Meditating with Aromatics

freesia, hyacinth, honeysuckle

Chapter Five: Less Ordinary Aromatics

Exploring less familiar but readily available scents

May include: All spice, patchouli, white sage, rose, lemon balm, eucalyptus, seaweed, cloves, cinnamon, cedar wood and sandalwood

Chapter Six: Exotics

Using exotic substances (but all available through mail order or from specialist shops)

May include: Frankincense, benzoin, amber, myrrh, storax, labdanum, spikenard, sandarac, dragon's blood, elemi, jasmine, neroli, opoponax, colophony

Chapter Seven: Seasonal/Festival Scents

Using seasonally available scented substances to enhance meditation through the year

May include: Snow and ice for January, snowdrops or hyacinth for February, narcissus or daffodils for March, lilac or violets for April, may blossom for May, roses or elder for June, elder or linden for July, strawberries or honeysuckle for August, hay or pencils and paper (back to school!) for September, apples or pumpkin for October, bonfire or toffee apples for November and clove-orange, mulled wine spices or pine for December

Chapter Eight: Scents for Sleep Meditations

Specially selected soporific scents and words for meditations to aid

Meditating with Aromatics

sleep and dreaming

May include: Lavender, hops, chamomile, clary sage

Chapter Nine: Where to go from here

Suggestions for own explorations

Feedback reports from "guinea pigs"

I aim to have a small selection of friends write a little about their experiences using the meditations

Chapter Ten: Sources

Bibliography (suggested reading, sources for materials, helpful websites)

Afterword: About the author

Short biography and thanks

Meditating with Aromatics

Meditating with Aromatics

Everyday Aromatics

Introduction

Not all aromatics are unfamiliar and exotic; many we take for granted our ancestors would have paid extortionate prices for. The beauty of the everyday aromatics is they are familiar and accessible; they are usually not expensive too, which makes them a good place to start.

The familiarity of the aromatics included in this chapter is also helpful in terms of ensuring before you start that you like the smell and that you do not have any allergies or sensitivities (physical, mental or emotional) that would make exploring the aromatic journey with that scent a hazardous or unpleasant experience.

It's worth repeating earlier advice about making sure you follow the suggested procedure for relaxing and getting into a meditative frame of mind and being sure to ground yourself afterwards by eating and drinking something. Be sure you are fully alert and aware before driving or performing any other potentially hazardous tasks. If you choose to record your experiences, it's worth writing them down both immediately after you finish the meditation and also later when you have had time to mull it all over. Insights may emerge days later too. Keep a special notebook for this; in it you can chart your experiences and challenges.

Because many of the aromatics in this chapter are so familiar, you may well find that after a few meditations with that substance, when you chance upon it in normal daily life, you may remember your experiences. This is something that I hope will enhance your daily life and make even simple acts such as slicing bread and making coffee into something that deepens your inner life and provides small oases of peace and tranquillity in a busy day.

Some of the aromatics in this chapter are available as dried herbs or

Meditating with Aromatics

as essential oils, and if for whatever reason you prefer to use them in that form, please refer back to my notes on vaporising oils or burning herbs and incense. Very few dried herbs smell terribly good when burned on charcoal; in fact, they usually smell like a garden bonfire or a smouldering compost heap. This will probably not be the effect you are looking for!

All the meditations have a period where the guidance stops for a while. How long is entirely up to you; this is your time to explore where the scent has led you, and this is where your experience will be yours and yours alone. You can use some form of alarm if you are unsure of being able to "wake up" but make sure it is not one that will startle you; the quiet beep of a digital watch is probably more than enough! At the end of the book there will be a few selected passages written by people who have used the mediations and have been kind enough to share their experiences. These are not goals or templates but simply someone else's journey using these meditations; your experience may be very different or it may be similar.

Remember, this is not a competition or an ordeal. If you become unduly uncomfortable with a meditation, allow yourself to come out of it and try and understand what was making you uncomfortable. You can always return to it another time. Insights will emerge, and so too will memories. I wrote extensively in the second chapter about how the sense of smell is in many ways the most powerful of our senses and the one we understand the least. Be gentle with yourself and never try and force yourself into places or memories you are not ready to visit. If you have serious problems occurring, it may well be best to postpone your exploration of that scent until you have found help. Try a different scent, one you are more comfortable with and remember that even with scents that have bad or unhelpful connotations, it is possible to overlay them with better ones. Healing of memories is not about wiping them from your mind but about taking away the negative and replacing it with something more positive.

Meditating with Aromatics

The following meditations are not set in order of difficulty; it's a very personal matter of which you choose to try first. Some you may find you use frequently and some may never be tried at all. Read the background information first and then read briefly though the meditation to see if it appeals to you today. You don't need to memorise it exactly but try and hold the narrative in your mind. You may like to record your own voice reading it slowly and play it back to yourself. If you prefer, allow your eyes to remain open and focussed softly on the words. When you have used the meditations a number of times, the balancing act between needing to read the words and needing to enter the meditation fully will become easier and more natural. Be gentle with yourself; if you find it easier to work with eyes open, then do that. It's all about you and how you want to work.

Meditating with Aromatics

Meditating with Aromatics

Everyday Aromatics

Meditation One: Orange

Background

To a modern person there is nothing terribly exciting about an orange but historically, for everyone but the very rich or the royal, the orange was a highly prized commodity and every part of it was used. Discarded peel was not thrown away but was dried to add to pot pourri or was candied to add to cakes, or was ground up and used in medicines. The vitamin rich fruit was until quite recently extremely expensive and hard to come by; those lucky children who found one at the foot of their Christmas stocking would have been more excited and pleased about it than any modern child can now imagine.

The sweet scent of an orange being peeled can lighten and freshen the atmosphere of a room and is especially helpful during the winter when its flesh and its fragrance can help ward off colds and also the blues.

For this meditation you will need either an orange (or Satsuma or other small citrus fruit) or you may use essential oil of orange placed either on an oil burner near where you are to sit, or a single drop on a strip of blotting paper.

Using the techniques described in chapter 3, begin to relax and enter a receptive state. When you feel comfortable, using a fingernail or a paring knife, scrape along the very top surface of the orange skin releasing the volatile oil. Hold the orange close to your face so that the aroma of the wounded skin can reach your nostrils without having to touch your skin. Breathe in the scent, slowly, allowing yourself to breathe normally, in through your nose and out through your mouth. Allow the fragrance to fill you.

13

Meditating with Aromatics

Now is the time to begin, still breathing steadily and softly allowing the scent of the orange to enter your nose and then your mind.

Meditation

You are standing amid a grove of mature orange trees, their trunks thick and strong. Through the canopy of branches you can see a brilliant blue sky, without a hint of a cloud anywhere, and the sun shines fiercely down, baking the ground to brick hardness. It is very still and distantly, beyond the trees you can see the shimmer of a deeper blue, telling you that you are not very far from the sea. Crickets sing but the birds have all sought shelter from the heat of the sun.

Walk deeper into the grove. The thick leathery leaves provide some protection from the intense sunshine, but when you look closer at some of the lower branches you can see that the leaves are dry and coated with a fine white dust. When you look at your feet as you slowly walk along, you can see little puffs of pale dust rising each time you set your feet down.

Look up at the trees. They are covered in both flowers and fruit and the scent of the flowers in particular is intoxicating, but the flowers are beginning to look slightly dry too, and the fruits are not as big or as juicy looking as you might imagine. Under the trees a little grass grows but it is looking tired and dusty too. You'd like to sit down but the grass looks uninviting. Walk a little further.

As you go deeper into the grove, the air grows heavier with both heat and fragrance, but the shade is very welcome and as you walk you see a bench built around the trunk of one of the oldest trees. The bench curves beautifully to encircle the orange tree; the wood is polished to a soft sheen by countless years of use. This is where the workers sit to take their ease and enjoy refreshment during the day. There is no one here now so approach the bench.

14

Meditating with Aromatics

On a small earthenware plate lies a pearl handled knife and an orange that one of the workers cut in half to eat and then left to seek the coolness of the farmhouse a short distance away. Sit down near the plate; the worker is fast asleep and will not be returning soon.

The bench is surprisingly comfortable, low and broad in the seat and the supporting back is angled so you can lean back a little and peer into the branches of the tree and see bright glimpses of the blue of the sky above. The scent of the opened orange rises to greet you and is incredibly refreshing and relaxing all at the same time. It cuts through the heavy scent of the flowers and dust.

Make yourself comfortable on the bench. I will leave you here for a while to enjoy the rest and the shade and the fragrance.

*

You are brought back to awareness by a change in the air. The light has changed too and as you look at the ground, a single immense drop of rain falls onto the ground and sends up a tiny cloud of dust. A second drop and then a third falls. Finally, the dry spell is being broken by the much-needed rain.

Stand up and begin walking back the way you entered the grove. Even through the thick canopy of leaves, the rain still strikes you, but it is warm rain and very pleasant after the oppressive heat and unrelenting sun. Pretty soon you are wet through. It's a nice feeling, like a warm shower.

As you leave the grove, stop a moment and turn back and look. Each leaf has been washed clean of the white dust of high summer, and all the fruits seem to be swelling and growing before your eyes, their skins clean and vibrant with the new rain. The flowers seem to perk up, their scent changed by the falling rain into something lighter,

15

Meditating with Aromatics

fresher and sweeter. The grass below the trees is also looking better, though the dust is turning to soft mud like a milky wash of clay.

Turning back, there is a faint rainbow in the sky, shining, and a rumble of distant thunder encourages you to seek shelter. The drumming of the rain on hard earth continues as you return now to your room and to full consciousness. Breathe deeply a few times and open you eyes. You are back.

Meditating with Aromatics

Exotics

Meditation One: Sandalwood

Background

Sandalwood is obtained as you might guess from the wood of an exotic tree. Most sandalwood plantations are in India, though some colonies have been planted in Australia. The wood has been used for statues, beads and incense for thousands of years and the essential oil is used extensively in both aromatherapy and in Ayurvedic medicine. It has a sweet and woody aroma that is very persistent; like frankincense it is used to slow and deepen the breathing to aid meditation. It is available as essential oil but can be expensive and it can be hard to obtain high quality oil. It is also available quite readily in the form of incense sticks (joss sticks) but the same caution applies here. Many joss sticks are named Sandalwood that have very little or no sandalwood present in them and while they may smell pleasant, they will have few of the beneficial effects offered by sticks made using high quality ingredients. The wood is sometimes available as shavings or chips and may be smouldered on charcoal to release the scent. If you are lucky enough to possess beads made from sandalwood, they release the scent when warmed by the body. The daughter of a good friend brought me some beads back from India recently and I love wearing them in hot weather as they continuously emit glorious but subtle wafts of fragrance as my body heat warms them.

For this meditation I recommend using a stick of sandalwood incense. If you have problems with smoke, light the stick in the room you intend to use for your meditation and once the stick has burned for ten or so minutes, put it out and leave the room for a further ten minutes to allow the smoke but not the aroma to dissipate. Then return to your room and shut the door. Make yourself comfortable and begin your preparations for meditation. When you are ready,

Meditating with Aromatics

relax and breathe deeply of the fragrance in the air.

Meditation

You are standing in a narrow street, surrounded by old buildings. There doesn't seem to be anyone around right now and the street is very quiet and empty. The road is paved with cobblestones made shiny with centuries of feet polishing them. In front of you is a half-timbered shop with a low door and two wide windows on either side of the door. The door is slightly open and you can smell a lovely fragrance of sandalwood; indeed you can see a fine thread of smoke curling through the opening. This is very inviting and you step forward and push the door open and peer inside. Just inside the door a stick of incense is burning, filling the air with scented smoke. The shop appears to be deserted so step inside and look around you.

The shop is a fabulous emporium of arts, crafts and gifts from all around the world. For a moment, you stand entranced, unable to take it all in. There are so many things that attract the eye. Glass cases are filled with imaginative displays of jewellery, all lovingly created and set out to their best advantage. Hopi and Navajo silver lie alongside Celtic brooches set with amber. Statues are dotted around on shelves, carved from wood and bone or moulded from clay or resins. Take your time to look around and see what is there.

There's a finely carved bookcase filled with rows of books. Some are empty journals, meant for you to write down your thoughts, though the majority are filled with the wisdom of a dozen or more cultures and philosophies. Take a moment to look through the titles and see if there is anything there that appeals to you. You may return later to the books if you choose.

Deeper into the shop, you see boxes of all different sizes and shapes, made from all different materials. Polished and worked silver and rough wooden boxes sit side by side, their lids a little open to invite

Meditating with Aromatics

you to see what they contain. Each box holds a different treasure; go and see for yourself what is in them.

You have the shop entirely to yourself today; you may look at anything you wish to. When you touch them, the locked glass display cabinets open for you. You may take out and handle whatever you like. You are trusted here.

When you have finished exploring the main body of the shop, walk further back and you will see there is a heavy crimson velvet curtain at the back. Pinned to it is a sign that says, "Welcome!" If you choose to, you may go through this curtain and see what is through there waiting to welcome you. If you prefer not to, then please go on exploring the wonders of the main shop or return to the books to browse further. I will return in a little while.

*

It's time to go now so step out of the shop and into the street again. There are people bustling around, so leave the door ajar so that the scent can invite someone else in. In your hand there is a parcel; this is the gift from the shop to you. Take a moment or two to see what you have been given and then allow yourself to return to the room where you began your meditation.

Meditating with Aromatics

Meditating with Aromatics

Seasonal/Festivals

Meditation One: New Year Meditation (Madonna Lily)

This mediation is intended to help review the year that has just passed and prepare for the new one about to start. If you are a regular meditator, go through your usual routine of preparation. The fragrance for this meditation is that of the lily so if you are lucky enough to have a bunch of lilies to hand, place them somewhere close so you can inhale their lovely scent. This is not essential to the meditation but may help if you feel the need.

Find somewhere quiet and comfortable and sit down. Make sure your back is straight and your legs are uncrossed.

Close your eyes and breathe in slowly. Hold the breath for a moment and then let it out again slowly. Do this a few times until you feel calm and centred.

You are standing in an ancient building. The stone flags beneath your feet are worn to a sheen by generations of feet that have walked upon them and the walls are thick. The few windows are small and set quite high in the walls and as your eyes get used to the dimness, you see that you are in a tiny church or chapel. It looks to be at least a thousand years old and you are the only person present. Here and there, clusters of candles burn, giving a glow of golden light. The scent of lilies is heavy in the air and arrangements of the flowers are stationed around the church. Facing east, you see that the altar has a simple pottery vase containing a few stems of lilies, illuminated by the group of beeswax candles nearby.

As you walk towards the altar, you see a casket standing on trestles in front of the altar and you realise with a sense of shock that you are here for a funeral. The casket is open and as you draw near and steel yourself to look, you see that it is empty. This is the funeral for the year that has just passed, your year and you are here to review its life in its entirety. Next to the casket is a bag, and you reach inside. It is packed with snapshot photographs, each one representing a moment, a day, a memory from the year that has passed. Some you smile at, some you feel tears welling up. One by one, gaze at each photo and allow yourself to remember, but without judgement. When you feel ready, drop the photo into the casket.

When each photo reaches the floor of the casket, a transformation takes place. Each memory changes into a precious stone, a jewel. The bright joyful memories become stones like sparkling diamonds or light blue sapphires or golden amber; the darker, more painful memories become jewels like polished onyx, blood red rubies or perhaps sapphires so deep blue they seem almost black. Observe each memory as it is transformed; some may surprise you what they become.

Once the bag of photos is empty, look closely at the jewels that now cover the floor of the casket. Give the casket a little shake and see how the stones shift around and make patterns. They seem to form groups of related memories, and it seems also that the darker stones give the lighter ones a deeper shine and the lighter ones make the dark ones sparkle. You can still identify which memory is which; if you wish, you may pick a few up and examine them more closely now they are transformed.

*

The time has come to say goodbye and you must shut the lid of the casket. As you do so, you see now that it is not a coffin as you had thought, but rather a treasure chest made of polished cedar, with a domed lid carved with beautiful patterns. Take the chest now and carry it towards the altar. You will see that the altar bears symbols that are special to you, and you feel happy to place your treasure chest of memories beneath it. It will be safe here and you can revisit

Meditating with Aromatics

and ponder the meaning of your treasures any time you choose but now it is time to go.

Walk back down the nave. The worn stones under your feet feel comforting but you have a sense of emptiness as one so often does after a funeral. The old year is gone and the new one is yet to begin; you are suspended between times now, just for this short time. It's a little uncomfortable because now you are starting to worry about what the new year will bring.

Close to the door there stands a great stone basin, a font of immense antiquity. The carvings around the bowl of it are worn but you can see patterns similar to those on the lid of your treasure chest. On the rim, flanked by groups of candles is another vase of lilies. You can smell their sweet fresh fragrance and as you watch, some of the powdery red pollen spills onto the surface of the water that fills the font. The powder spreads out and you watch fascinated as the play of candlelight and reflections make pictures come alive in the water and you realise that you are seeing scenes from what the new year may bring. Watch, but without judgement or attachment; these are things that may happen. Nothing is certain yet. Just as the previous year had good and bad in it, so too will the next one.

The great battered door, armoured with blackened iron swings open a little and the breeze scatters the pollen and the pictures cease. You walk towards the door and glance back. At the altar, the lilies still glow golden in the light from the candle flames and your treasure chest nestles beneath in the dancing shadows. The water on the font ripples with the wind that enters and shakes the flames like leaves on a tree and you know it is time to leave this place.

Outside, you can feel the changes that have taken place and the first rays of light of a new dawn turn the sky a heavenly pink, and you know that this new day heralds a new year full of joys and sorrows, and you step forth, determined to understand the treasure in both.

Meditating with Aromatics

Meditating with Aromatics

Seasonal Meditations

March: Narcissus

Background

The narcissus is a member of the daffodil family and has been bred to produce some spectacularly pretty spring flowers. The usual colours are shades of yellow, and cream, though others have been produced in other combinations. They usually bloom throughout the early spring and are often on sale in pots having been 'forced' to bloom a little earlier than they do naturally.

The scent of the narcissus is very sweet and almost hypnotic. It is available as an absolute, but is very expensive and aromatherapy books advise caution when using it as it is considered somewhat narcotic in effect and can be toxic.

The flower is named after a handsome youth in Greek myth who fell in love with his own reflection in a forest pool. Unable to reach the beautiful image, he pined away and died, and the flower sprang up where his body lay. The various different versions of the story all reflect a moral of avoiding self-obsession, though the details of both the events and the outcome change from one version to another. This meditation is aimed at promoting both understanding and love for the inner self.

To do the meditation I would suggest buying some ready prepared bulbs in advance and waiting till they are in full bloom. You may also like to buy them as cut flowers, but buying them as bulbs means that you may plant them later and have a reminder as the bulbs grow and spread and flower every year thereafter. If you are unable to obtain the flower, you may use the absolute, placing a single drop on a strip of blotting paper.

If you can manage it, performing this meditation outdoors on a sunny day enhances the effect; sitting by a sunny window works well

Meditating with Aromatics

too, with the pot or vase of narcissus flowers in front of you. Go through your usual preparations of grounding and relaxing; breathe the sweet, intoxicating aroma of the flowers, letting the petals brush your face.

Meditation

Let the sweet scent fill your mind and feel the soft brush of the flowers against your skin.

The soft breeze touches your face and brings a fragrance of fresh leaves as well as that of the flowers. Sunlight dances through the newly opened leaves above you; each leaf is still soft and crumpled from the bud. You are in a grove of trees, widely spaced and the grass below them is finely grown and neatly trimmed as if this were parkland and not wild meadows.

Spring flowers grow here and there but the strongest scent of all is coming from a short distance away. You can see an ornamental pool, perfectly round and encircled by smooth stone, coated with a soft layer of the deepest moss. At the four points of the compass there is a stone urn, fixed securely to the stone surround of the pool, and each of these is filled with narcissi in fullest bloom. Today they are at their very best; you have come at the perfect moment to see them and smell them.

Go over to the pool and walk around it, clockwise. It's a surprisingly large pool and it seems quite deep. A few deep green leaves from a water lily float on the dark surface of the water but it's far too early for the flowers. The fragrance of the narcissi floats on the mild spring air and bird song begins. A single flower head floats on the water.

It's very peaceful here and you sit down on the stone encircling the pool. The moss acts as a cushion, softening the stone for you. In the centre of the pool there is a statue that might well be a fountain,

26

Meditating with Aromatics

but the water is still today and the statue does not seem to cast a reflection. Then you notice that the water does not seem to be reflecting anything, not even the sky.

Lean out a little way and look into the water. What do you see in the water? Do you see yourself looking back? Do you like what you see? What would you change if you could? Let yourself have some time contemplating this.

A brisk wind rises and shakes the surface of the water and disperses the images you saw there, as if they were being wiped away by magic. You glimpse the bottom of the pool and maybe a goldfish or two before the breeze drops entirely and the surface of the water is completely still, and becomes mirror like. As you sit there, inhaling the sweet fragrance, let yourself gaze into the water. Who or what will appear there for you, now? I will let you spend as long as you need here.

*

You come back to yourself and see that the short spring day is drawing to a close, and the pool is now reflecting the sky as you would expect. The evening star has appeared, and shines as brightly in the water as in the sky and you know it is time to go back. As you look, the flowers seem to have faded already, past their best now though the scent is as sweet as ever.

As the daylight fades too and the evening sky turns to deep blue, walk back to where you started, leaving the lovely pool behind and when you are ready take a few deep breaths and open your eyes. You are now back.

Meditating with Aromatics

Meditating with Aromatics

Seasonal Meditations

February: Snowdrop

Background

For many people the snowdrop is the bringer of spring, the first of the true flowers of springtime. Blooming often when the snow is still on the ground, being blasted by gales, frozen by frosts and battered by rain, it is a witness to the unconquerable strength of nature. The tiny flowers hang like little white bells, their petals so fragile and yet they endure everything that the tail end of winter can throw at them. Few people ever kneel down to inhale their sweet, lily-like scent and so it remains a secret known only to a few.

The scent of the snowdrop is subtle and not easy to catch; outdoors the scent may rise on a still day in February, but days when the wind doesn't blow are few in that cold month. For this meditation I suggest planning ahead and buying or planting some snowdrop bulbs in pot, or if you have them growing in your garden, pick a handful and place them in a small vase with water and watch for them beginning to open their flowers properly. The scent will not emerge from unopened buds and so this is a seasonal meditation where you may have only a few short days or hours where it is possible to do it. If you are lucky and have the unusual combination of a sunny and still day, a location with plentiful snowdrops and sufficient privacy to meditate, then the meditation may be done outdoors. There is no essential oil of snowdrop, to my knowledge, and they do now retain much, if any scent when dried.

The arrival of the snowdrops is for me the turning point of the winter, when however much bad weather arrives after that, I have seen the spring starting. If you suffer from Seasonally Affective Disorder (SAD), the return of the light is very important both physically and psychologically. There is a flower essence available

Meditating with Aromatics

that may help with this, and may be useful taken before this meditation, if you find that Energy Medicine is helpful to you.

Follow the usual grounding and relaxing processes and then place your pot or vase of snowdrops close to your chosen seat, and for a few moments gaze at the flowers. Lift the flowers close to your face; feel the petals brush your skin as if the breeze were shaking them and inhale slowly and deeply. The fragrance will rise softly as the flowers warm; it comes in waves, sometimes barely there, other times quite strong. Wait until you have smelled the fragrance a few times and then begin.

Meditation

The pale yellow sun of earliest spring is pouring through the bare twigs and branches of ancient woodland. You are standing on the edge of a clearing; hazel and birch trees surround you and beyond them larger and older trees stand as sentinels. The clearing is filled with snowdrops among the rough clumps of grass, and they are at the very peak of their blooming. There is hardly any breeze, but every so often a tiny hint of wind shakes the tiny flower heads like a thousand miniature bells; you might almost hear them ring with a faint silvery tone. Their scent rises to greet you in waves, a little like that of lilies but not cloying and very fresh and exhilarating, like the spring breeze that shakes the flowers from time to time.

Watch the flowers quiver and dance when the wind gusts through the clearing; see how their petals gleam brilliantly white in the new sunshine. There is still frost on the ground here and there; some of the grasses are dusted with crystals of ice, but as you watch, these are melting and the bright drops of moisture glitter in the light.

Walk further into the clearing and you will see that the trees make and almost perfect circle around you. Somewhere in the bushes a wren is singing her spring song; a blackbird tunes up and then

Meditating with Aromatics

breaks into song too. You can hear the chuckle of running water too, but right now you can't see where it is coming from.

Stand for a moment in the middle of the clearing and very slowly turn round and look at what surrounds you. The trees are still bare of leaves but even from this distance you can see the swelling of the buds. It will be a while yet before the buds break and burst forth into full leaf, but the signs are there. Birds move from branch to branch, and you can hear them squabble as well as sing. Some even seem to be carrying nesting materials, though this seems far too early and far too cold to be egg- laying time yet.

At the edge of the clearing, you catch a glimpse of something that interests you. A low wall of ancient lichen-covered stones surrounds a small pool, from which emerges a narrow channel. The water flows from the pool and into the channel and then becomes a little stream, the bottom lined with shining pebbles. The snowdrops are so densely packed near this pool that it is hard to walk among them without stepping on them. When you get to the pool you can see that it is a spring, and the water is as pure and clear as you could wish for. Taste some; it is icy cold but very good. Around the low wall around the spring, someone has laid snowdrops, making a pattern of them. Look closely and see what the pattern seems to tell you. I will leave you here for a while to enjoy the scent of the flowers, the sunlight and the song of the spring.

*

A shadow seems to pass across the face of the sun; a wisp of cloud has been blown across it, bringing you back to the here and now. The wind is gathering strength, and there is moisture in the air as if rain is on its way, and it feels colder suddenly, reminding you that spring is still barely here. You feel it is time to go home. Inhale the scent of the snowdrops and feel them fill you with the energy to

31

Meditating with Aromatics

endure the rest of the time before the year turns more steadily to the sun. The quiet laughter of the spring beside you fills your heart with joy and as you pass from the flower filled glade and back into the room where you began, keep with you the feelings and thoughts the snowdrops gave you and keep them safe in your heart as the year warms. You are now back.

Meditating with Aromatics

Other Meditations

Crystal Cave

Background

For this meditation you may like to have a crystal to focus on; a geode works especially well. Remember to turn the phone off and make sure you are not going to be interrupted. Using either soft music or a natural sounds tape of perhaps a stream will enhance the experience but is not essential as long as you have reasonable quiet around you.

Meditation

Breathe slowly but without forcing it. Allow yourself to relax and become calm but alert. Let your eyes close naturally and become still.

You walking along in the cool air of an underground passage; the tunnel is lit with softly flickering candles in niches along the walls. The sweet smell of beeswax reaches you every time you pass a niche and your movement causes the candlelight to flicker. It's very peaceful here and you sense that many people have come along here before; it's totally safe. The carefully smoothed walls of the tunnel glisten and gleam in the candlelight; when you touch them they are slightly damp and slippery to the touch.

Continue along; the floor slopes steadily but not alarmingly and after a while you come to an opening ahead of you where a light gleams. Go through the opening. You are in a large cave, lit only by candlelight. A single candle floats in a pool of very clear water in the centre of the cave. It seems far lighter in here than you might expect

Meditating with Aromatics

from just one candle and you look round for the reason.

The whole cave is lined with the finest and most lovely crystals you can imagine. You are inside a living geode, a bubble of earth where crystals have grown for centuries. The light from the single candle is reflected from each facet of the tens of thousands of crystals that cover every inch of the walls and ceiling of the cave.

It's simply breathtaking.

You sit down near the pool of water, there is a low stool carved from oak and you find it very comfortable. As you sit and marvel and the cave, you notice something else. The pool of water is not still; bubbles rise steadily from the centre and you see now that water softly spills over one end of the natural stone bowl, and into a groove in the floor where it trickles away with a lovely sound like living music.

Sit quietly and enjoy the radiance of the earth-born crystals and the music of the earth-born waters. The air is cool and fresh and moist and any difficulties you may have had with breathing vanish in this pure healing air. You feel deeply peaceful and at one with the earth. Touch the water and scoop a little in your hand and bathe your face with it; feel the worries and cares melt away.

Stay as long as you wish, feeling the deep healing this place gives to any who visit, and when you feel it is time to return to the outer world, whisper your prayers to the cave. They will be heard.

As you leave, your movement sets the candle flickering and the light dances and casts rainbows across your face.

Return up the stone passage way and find yourself back where you began. Breathe deeply and when you are ready open your eyes. You are home.

Meditating with Aromatics

Notes

www.ingramcontent.com/pod-product-compliance
Lightning Source LLC
Chambersburg PA
CBHW071802020426
42331CB00008B/2368